ULTIMATE
HIDDEN PICTURES
ACROSS AMERICA
TONY AND TONY TALLARICO

PSS!
PRICE STERN SLOAN

Also available:
Ultimate Hidden Pictures on Halloween
Ultimate Hidden Pictures Under the Sea

ISBN 978-0-8431-0265-9

HOOVER DAM

At over 726 feet tall, this historic landmark is one of the top construction achievements of the 20th century.

☐☐Balloons (2) ☐Binoculars ☐☐Birds (2) ☐Boom box ☐Clown ☐Fish
☐Fishing pole ☐Ghost ☐Ice-cream cone ☐Necktie ☐Paper airplane ☐Plunger
☐Santa Claus ☐Soccer ball ☐Suspenders ☐Teddy bear ☐Toothbrush ☐Watering can

MOVIE & TV STUDIO TOUR

Did you ever watch a movie or television program and wonder what goes on behind the scenes?

- ☐ Astronaut
- ☐ Bicycle
- ☐ Birdcage
- ☐ Bone
- ☐ Bowling ball
- ☐ Clipboard
- ☐ Cook
- ☐ Crown
- ☐ Dunce cap
- ☐ Hamburger
- ☐☐ Hearts (2)
- ☐ Hockey stick
- ☐ Juggler
- ☐ Magnifying glass
- ☐ Mail carrier
- ☐ Mummy
- ☐ Pirate
- ☐ Robot
- ☐ Sherlock Holmes
- ☐ Snake
- ☐ Snowman
- ☐ Star
- ☐ Stretch limousine
- ☐ Sunglasses
- ☐ Surfboard
- ☐ Sword
- ☐ Turtle
- ☐ TV set
- ☐ Unicycle

SUNNY CALIFORNIA BEACHES

Enjoy the Pacific Ocean and the sandy beaches of the Golden State!

☐ Anchor ☐ Baseball cap ☐ Beach ball ☐ Bird ☐ Boom box ☐ Cat ☐ Coonskin cap ☐ Escaped convict ☐ Flying saucer ☐ Hot dog ☐ Key ☐ Kite ☐ Lost key ☐ Lunchbox ☐ Mermaid ☐ Moon crest ☐ Moustache ☐ Shark fin ☐ Shovel ☐ Skates ☐ Snake ☐☐ Stars (2) ☐☐ Sunglasses (2) ☐ Top hat ☐ Turtle ☐☐ Umbrellas (2) ☐ Walking stick ☐ Water skier ☐ Whale ☐ Who is wearing "flippers"?

CAMPING AT YELLOWSTONE NATIONAL PARK

Are these campers really prepared to spend time in this famous landmark?

☐Arrow ☐Balloon ☐Bone ☐Butterfly ☐Camera ☐Canteen ☐Cheese ☐Coffeepot ☐Coyote ☐Eyeglasses ☐Flashlight ☐Ghost ☐Golfer ☐Grizzly bear ☐Guitar ☐Key ☐Kite ☐Heart ☐Lost sock ☐Moustache ☐Oar ☐☐Owls (2) ☐Scissors ☐☐☐☐Snakes (4) ☐Pumpkin ☐Rabbit ☐Turtle ☐TV antenna

WINTER FUN IN COLORADO

Skiing and snowboarding are great activities... but not for these enthusiasts.

☐Baseball cap ☐Basketball ☐Beach ball ☐Birdhouse ☐Cactus
☐DEAD END sign ☐☐Earmuffs (2) ☐Flying bat ☐Flying saucer ☐Igloo
☐ONE WAY sign ☐Periscope ☐Pizza delivery ☐Practical joker ☐Reindeer
☐Santa ☐Satellite dish ☐Scarecrow ☐☐☐Scarves (3) ☐Sled ☐Star
☐Top hat ☐TV set ☐Umbrella
☐Yo-yo ☐☐☐☐☐Who doesn't ski (5)

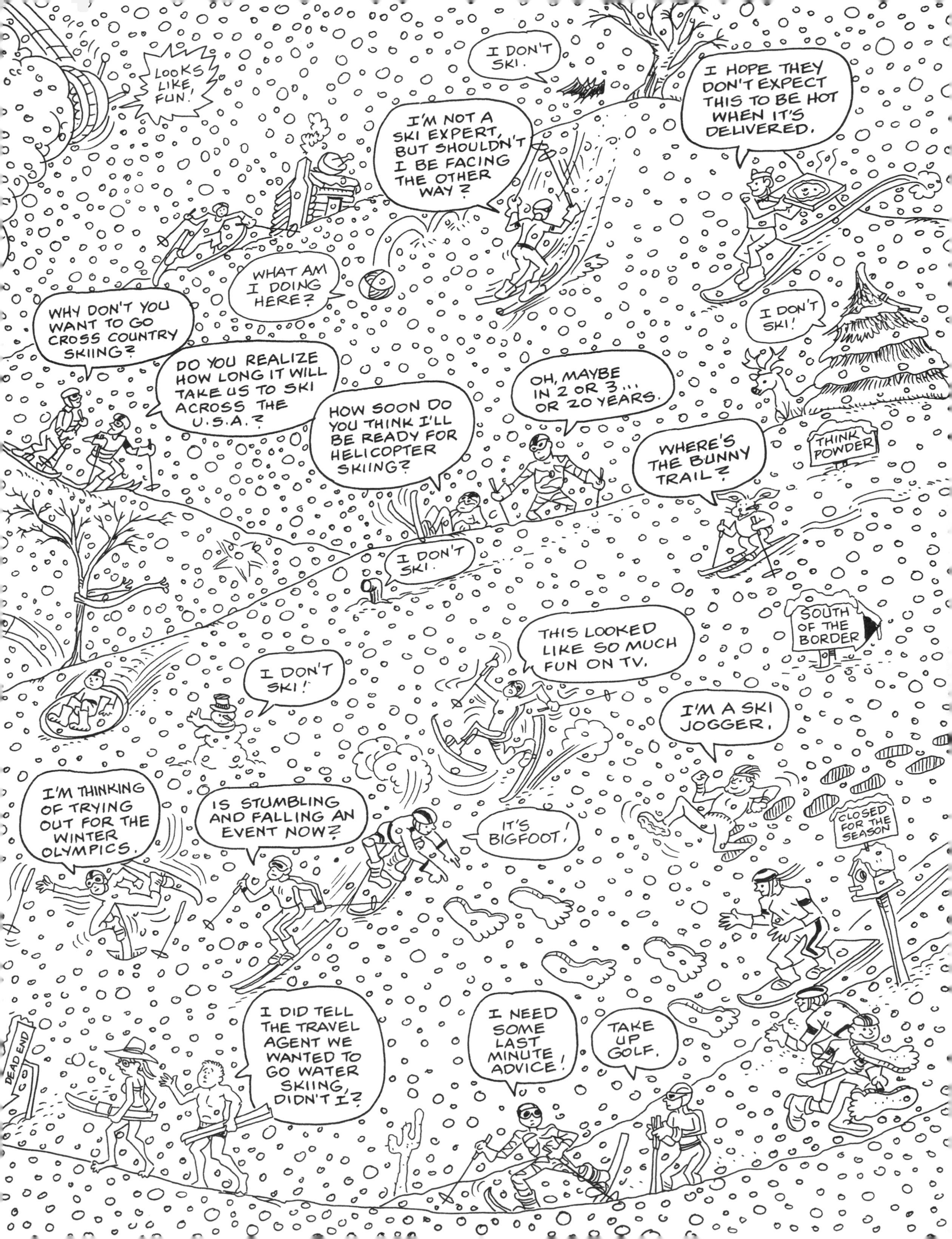
LOOKS LIKE FUN!
I DON'T SKI.
I'M NOT A SKI EXPERT, BUT SHOULDN'T I BE FACING THE OTHER WAY?
I HOPE THEY DON'T EXPECT THIS TO BE HOT WHEN IT'S DELIVERED.
WHAT AM I DOING HERE?
WHY DON'T YOU WANT TO GO CROSS COUNTRY SKIING?
DO YOU REALIZE HOW LONG IT WILL TAKE US TO SKI ACROSS THE U.S.A.?
I DON'T SKI!
HOW SOON DO YOU THINK I'LL BE READY FOR HELICOPTER SKIING?
OH, MAYBE IN 2 OR 3... OR 20 YEARS.
WHERE'S THE BUNNY TRAIL?
THINK POWDER
I DON'T SKI.
SOUTH OF THE BORDER
THIS LOOKED LIKE SO MUCH FUN ON TV.
I DON'T SKI!
I'M A SKI JOGGER.
I'M THINKING OF TRYING OUT FOR THE WINTER OLYMPICS.
IS STUMBLING AND FALLING AN EVENT NOW?
IT'S BIGFOOT!
CLOSED FOR THE SEASON
DEAD END
I DID TELL THE TRAVEL AGENT WE WANTED TO GO WATER SKIING, DIDN'T I?
I NEED SOME LAST MINUTE ADVICE!
TAKE UP GOLF.

A SPECTACULAR SITE

You'll need an amazing wide angle lens to take a snapshot of
this famous Arizona landmark!

☐Apple ☐Artist ☐Backpack ☐Balloon ☐Bear ☐Binoculars ☐Bird
☐☐Bottles of water (2) ☐☐☐Cactus (3) ☐☐☐Canteens (3) ☐Chef's hat ☐Clown
☐Flying saucer ☐Football ☐Ghost ☐Guitar ☐Hot dog ☐Ice-cream cone ☐Key
☐Lost sneaker ☐Paper airplane ☐Pick ☐Snake ☐Skunk ☐Uncle Sam ☐Yo-yo

REMEMBER THE ALAMO!

This historic complex in San Antonio, Texas, attracts more than 2.5 million visitors a year.

☐☐☐Backpacks (3) ☐Barrel ☐Butterfly ☐Cactus ☐Canteen ☐Dog
☐Eyeglasses ☐Hammer ☐Horseshoe ☐Ice-cream cone ☐Necktie
☐Overalls ☐Pencil ☐Roller skates ☐Sailor cap ☐Saw
☐Snake ☐☐☐☐☐☐Stars (6) ☐☐☐☐Ten gallon hats (4)
☐Teepee ☐Toothbrush ☐Umbrella

MARDI GRAS TIME!

It's the granddaddy of all New Orleans festivals.

☐☐☐Aliens (3) ☐Ape ☐Bagpipe ☐Baseball cap ☐Beach ball
☐Bird ☐Brush ☐Candle ☐Cat ☐☐Drums (2) ☐Dunce cap
☐Flying bat ☐☐☐Ghosts (3) ☐Hot dog ☐Kangaroo ☐Kite
☐Lost key ☐Moustache ☐Pumpkin ☐Snake ☐Superhero
☐Top hat ☐Tuba player ☐Turtle ☐☐Umbrellas (2)
☐Vampire ☐Walrus

CONNECTING FLIGHTS

Before you can have that relaxing vacation...
you need to get through some craziness!

☐Astronaut ☐Apple ☐Backpack ☐Bare foot ☐Bell ☐Broom ☐Clown
☐Cell phone ☐Dog ☐☐☐Flower pots (3) ☐Mailbox ☐Mouse ☐Oil can
☐Pencil ☐Ponytail ☐Roller skates ☐Skis ☐Soda can ☐Sombrero
☐Star ☐Sunglasses ☐Superhero ☐Suspenders
☐☐Trash cans (2) ☐☐☐☐☐☐Who can fly without an engine? (6)

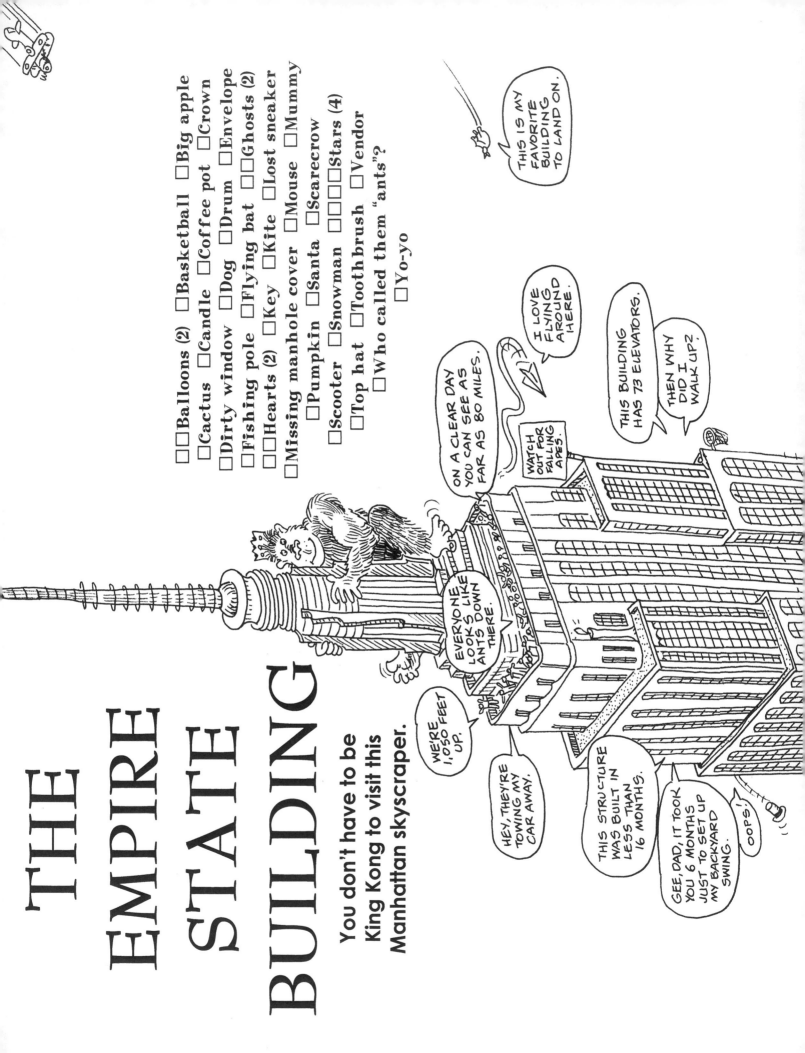

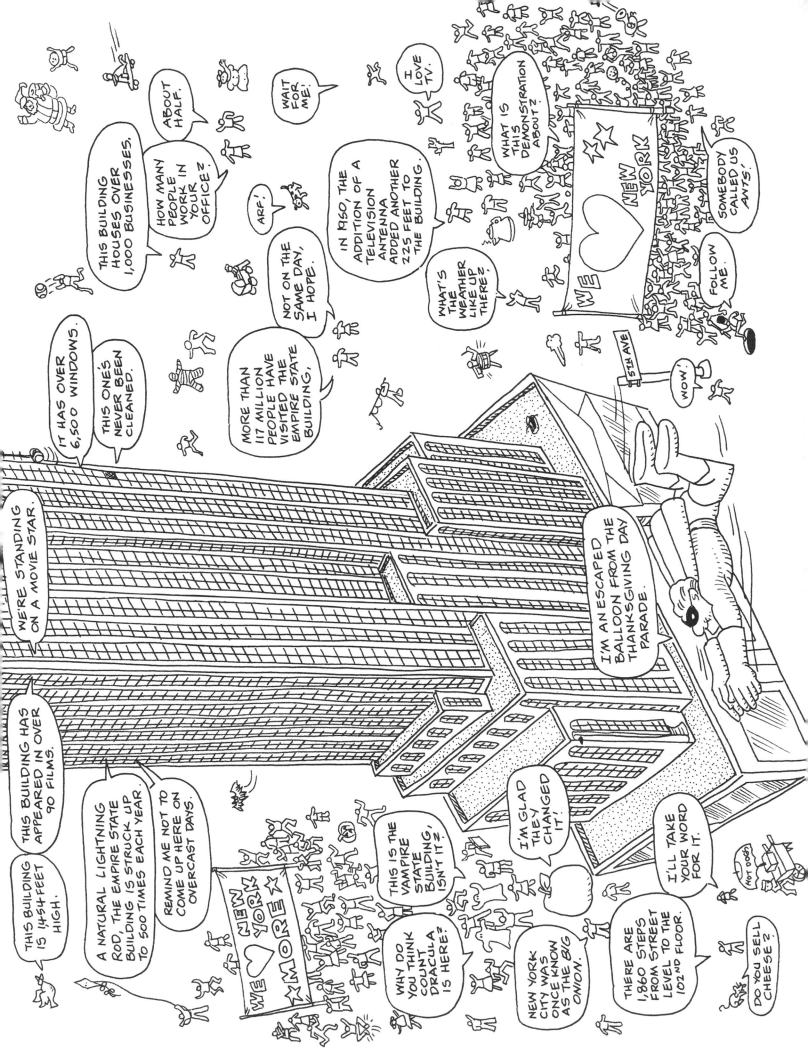

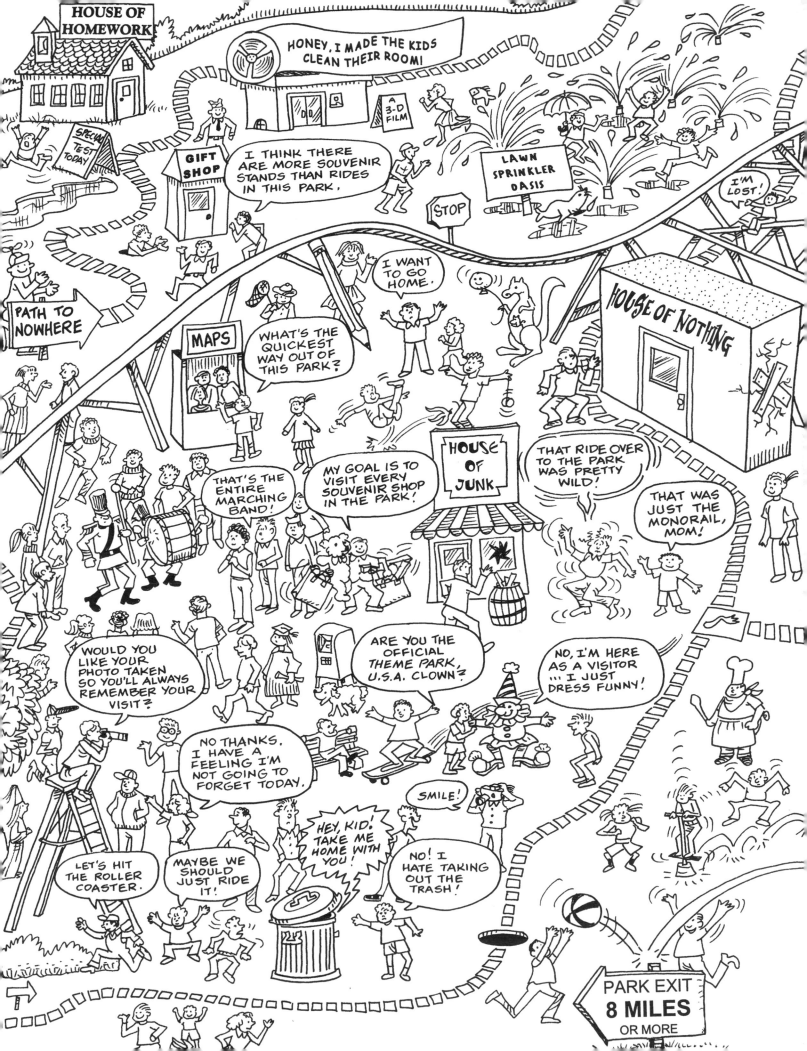

CLEVELAND ROCKS!

There's so much to do in this Ohio city ... you might not know where to go first!

☐Anchor ☐☐☐☐☐☐Balloons (6) ☐☐☐☐Banana peels (4) ☐Basketball hoop ☐Bat ☐☐Birds (2) ☐Boom box ☐Broken window ☐Broom ☐Cat ☐Cell phone ☐Clown ☐Eyeglasses ☐Flying saucer ☐Hard hat ☐Jack-o-lantern ☐Ladder ☐Mailbox ☐☐☐☐☐Neckties (5) ☐Paper airplane ☐Puddle ☐Saxophone player ☐Scarecrow ☐Skateboard ☐Sunglasses ☐☐Telescopes (2) ☐Top hat ☐☐Traffic cones (2) ☐☐Umbrellas (2) ☐Wristwatch ☐Wrong word sign

CAVERN ADVENTURES

A field trip below the earth's surface!

☐Apple ☐Candle ☐Cane ☐Dog bone ☐Drum ☐Duck ☐Envelope ☐Fish ☐Flower ☐☐Ghosts (2) ☐Giant rabbit ☐Hammer ☐Heart ☐Horseshoe ☐Igloo ☐Kite ☐Lamp ☐Lost sock ☐Mouse ☐Pumpkin ☐Ring ☐Skateboard ☐Skull ☐Star ☐Toaster ☐Tombstone ☐Top hat ☐TV set ☐Vampire ☐Wristwatch

ROCK CLIMBING IN NORTH CAROLINA

Which member of this team is the weakest link?

☐ Axe ☐ Book ☐ Bottle of water ☐ Candy cane
☐ Coffee pot ☐ Drum ☐ Drying laundry ☐ Duck
☐ Fish ☐ Flower ☐ Flying saucer ☐ Football
☐ Frog ☐ Guitar ☐ Hockey stick ☐ Kite
☐ Lost cooking pot ☐ Lost sock
☐ Paintbrush ☐ Paper airplane
☐ Pick ☐ Pencil ☐ Skunk
☐☐☐ Snakes (3)
☐ Spoon ☐☐ Stars (2)
☐ Toothbrush
☐ TV set ☐ Yo-yo

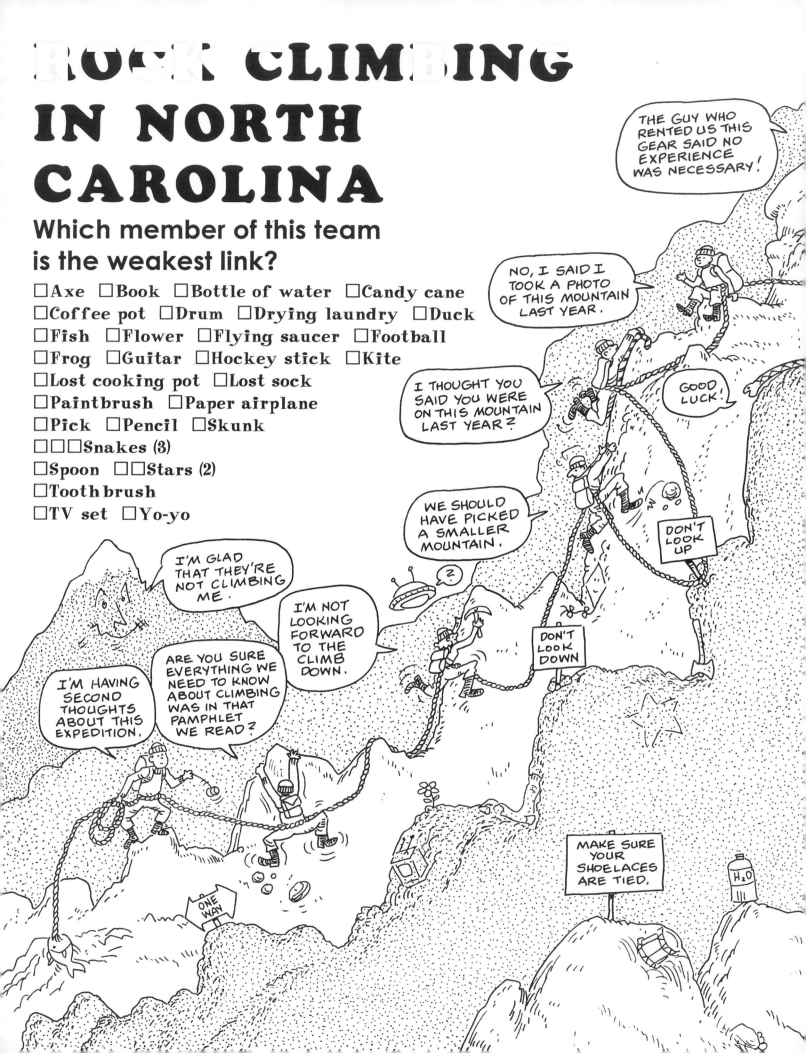

AN OUT OF THIS WORLD VISIT TO KENNEDY SPACE CENTER

A trip to Florida's space coast can be a lot of fun ... just don't touch any buttons!

☐ Alien ☐ Balloon ☐ Banana ☐ Baseball cap ☐ Briefcase ☐☐ Cameras (2) ☐ Candle
☐ Cell phone ☐ Coffee pot ☐ Cup ☐ Football ☐ Golf club ☐ Heart ☐ Key ☐ Kite
☐ Lost sock ☐ Magnet ☐☐ Mice (2) ☐☐☐☐ Palm trees (4) ☐ Pencil ☐ Pogo stick
☐ Pumpkin ☐ Rake ☐ Santa ☐ Snake ☐ Star ☐ Sunglasses ☐ Ten gallon hat
☐ Tin man ☐ Turtle ☐ Umbrella

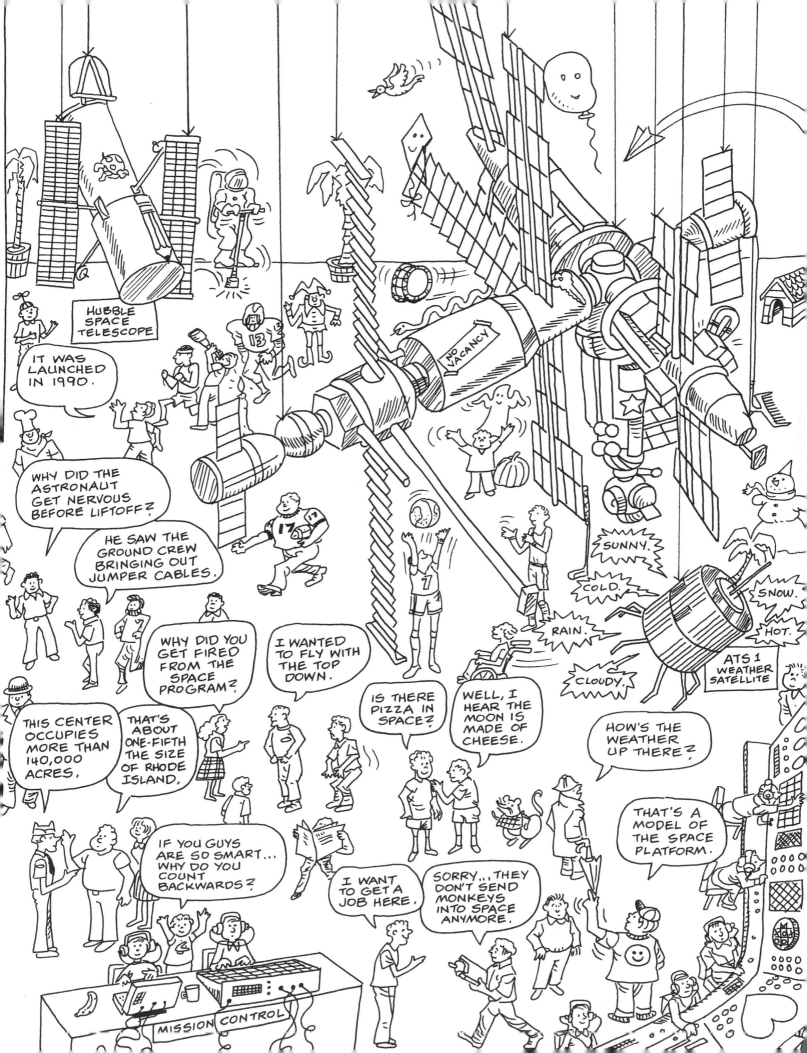

A CONNECTICUT SEAPORT

This charming east coast seaport is filled with history, fun activities...
and a few surprises!

☐Accident ☐Anchor ☐Barrel ☐Basketball ☐Bell ☐Bicycle ☐Chimney ☐Cook ☐Cow ☐Diver ☐Fish ☐Guitar ☐Jolly Roger ☐Key ☐Kite ☐Ladder ☐Mailbox ☐Necktie ☐Octopus ☐Rabbit ☐☐☐☐Seagulls (4) ☐Shopping bag ☐Skateboard ☐Sunglasses ☐Suspenders ☐Top hat ☐Trash can ☐☐Turtles (2) ☐TV antenna ☐Wheelchair

STEP BACK IN TIME TO COLONIAL AMERICA

Explore the 18th century with a walking tour of old Virginia.

☐Axe ☐Backpack ☐Balloon ☐☐Barrels (2) ☐Basket ☐Bell
☐☐☐Birds (3) ☐Book ☐Broom ☐Camera ☐Candle ☐Clock ☐Drummer
☐Duck ☐Eagle ☐Horse ☐Ice-cream cone ☐I LOVE VIRGINIA banner ☐Key
☐Kite ☐Lantern ☐Pencil ☐Ring ☐Rocking horse ☐Santa ☐Soccer ball
☐Untied shoelace

PUTTING IN PENNSYLVANIA

Miniature golf is a great way to spend time together. Just remember … it's not who wins or loses but how you play the game.

☐☐Baseball caps (2) ☐Bowling ball ☐Beret ☐Cannon ☐Drum
☐☐Fire hydrants (2) ☐Firecracker ☐Heart ☐Jack-o-lantern ☐Knight in armor
☐Lampshade ☐Lost golf ball ☐Mouse ☐Periscope ☐Roller skates ☐Saw ☐Shark fin
☐Skateboard ☐☐☐Stars (3) ☐Talking trash can ☐Traffic cone ☐Wobble glove ☐Worm

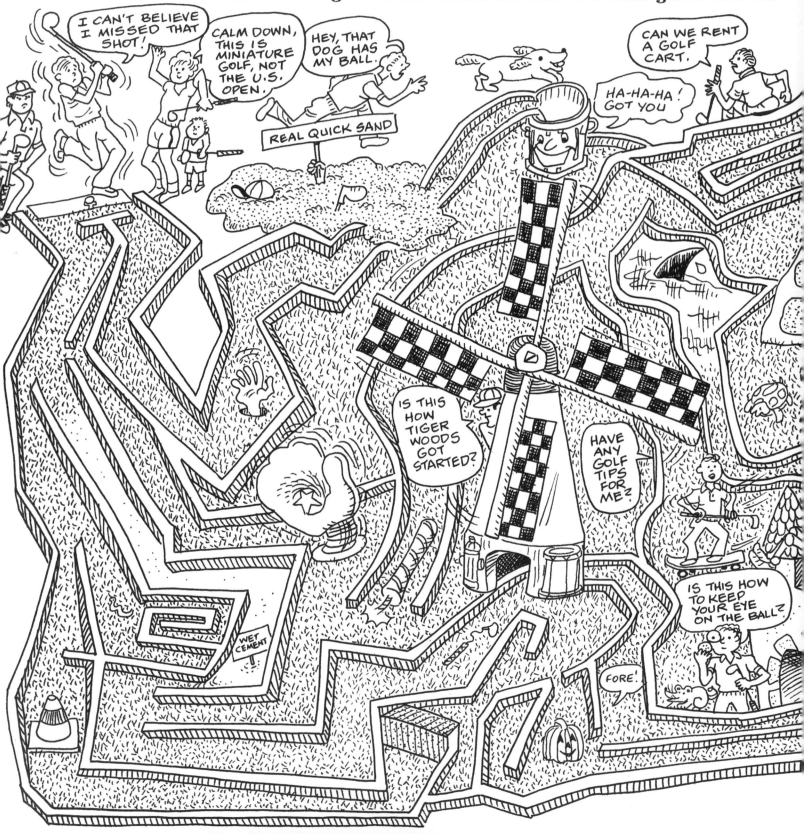

MUSEUM OF UNNATURAL HISTORY

A visit to a museum anywhere in our country is a day well spent ...
except of course at this museum.

☐☐ Band aids (2) ☐ Bell ☐ Bird ☐ Bone ☐ Butterfly ☐ Clock ☐ Coffee mug ☐ Cracked egg ☐ Dog ☐ Dunce cap ☐ Fish ☐ Flower pot ☐ Ice-cream cone ☐ Ice skate ☐ Mailbox ☐ Paintbrush ☐ Paper airplane ☐ Pie slice ☐ Plunger ☐ Scarecrow ☐ Spider web ☐ Star ☐ Suspenders ☐ Tire ☐ Toothbrush ☐ Toothpaste tube ☐ Wooden foot

THE BOSTON MARATHON

A run through the streets of Massachusetts is not for the typical couch potato!

☐Alien ☐Ape ☐Astronaut ☐☐☐Balloons (3) ☐Banana peel ☐Birdcage ☐Broom ☐Cell phone ☐Cook ☐Court Jester ☐Crown ☐Dunce cap ☐Elephant ☐Escaped convict ☐Fish ☐Flowerpot ☐Football player ☐Ghost ☐Horse ☐Hot dog ☐Kite ☐Lost sneaker ☐Lost sock ☐Moustache ☐Moose ☐Mummy ☐Penguin ☐Pumpkin ☐Santa ☐Scarf ☐Snake ☐Surfer ☐Superhero ☐Tennis racquet ☐Top hat ☐Tuba ☐Turtle ☐Umbrella ☐Vampire

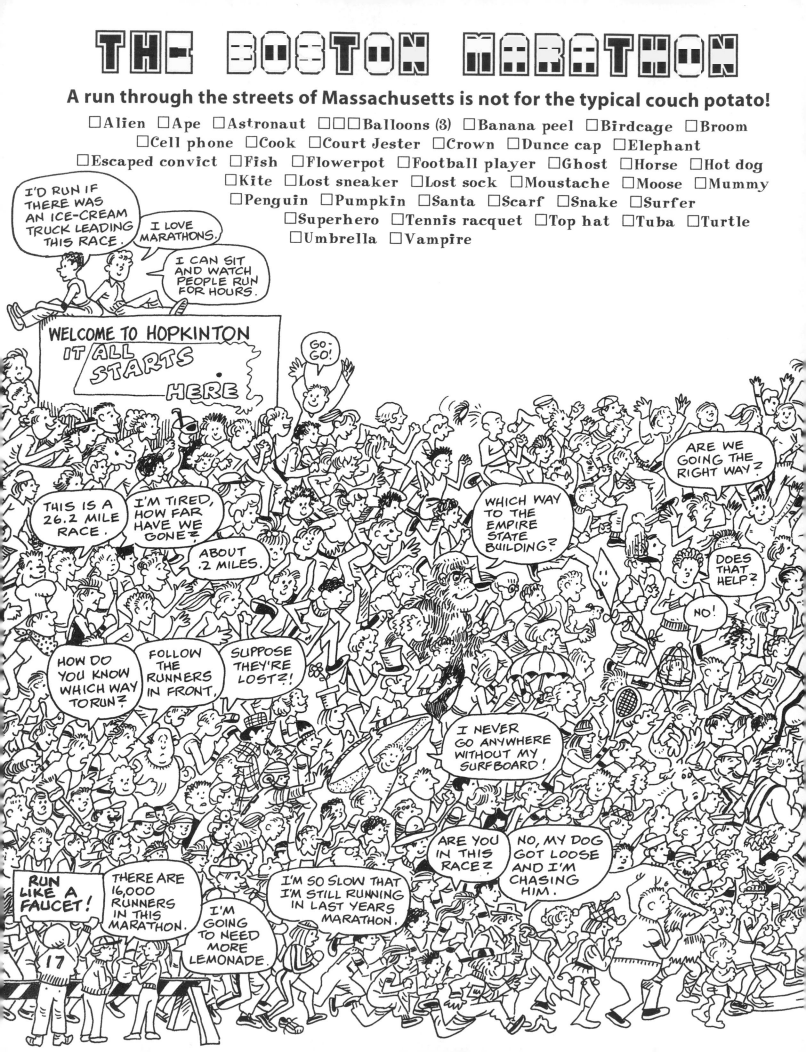